Giorgio Mobili

Sunken Boulevards

Fomite
Burlington VT

Copyright © 2021 Giorgio Mobili

All rights reserved. No part of this book may be reproduced in any form or by any means without the prior written consent of the publisher, except in the case of brief quotations used in reviews and certain other noncommercial uses permitted by copyright law.

ISBN: 978-1-953236-29-6
Library of Congress Control Number: 2021943143

Fomite
58 Peru Street
Burlington, VT 05401
www.fomitepress.com
9/13/2021

In loving memory of my mother

Carla Corti Mobili

Contents

The Scent of Tomorrow	3
What We Leave Behind	4
Lovers Gone Wrong	5
Go West	7
Revelation	11
Vacancy	13
Seasonal Heartbreak	15
Different Birds	16
Hinterland	17
Back To Bonera	19
Heartbreak Café	21
Sirens	23
China	25
Starve Game	27
Cocktails	28
Home	29
Crash Landing	33
Heatwave	35
Summer Songs	37
Intercom	39
Boundless Hotels	41
Sicilian Renaissance	43
Day of Reckoning	45
Tahiti	47
Closing Time	51
Victims of Stars	52
American Casanova	53
Chickens	55
Rekindling	57
Perfect Sleep	59
Feathers	61
The Grownup Years	63
The Call	65

Radioland	69
Night Ride	70
Black Heart	71
Diva	73
Night Song	75
Lockdown	76
Fear Of Heights	77
Friendly Fire	79
Boat of Return	81
Borderline	83
Horoscope	85
Summer Days	87
Night Chill	88
Nightwatchers	89
Pledge	91
Boys	93
Return To Villa Severi	97
Charcoal Beaches	99
Narrow Margins	101
Dark	102
Sunken Boulevards	103
Quinta Vergara	105
About the Author	107

Acknowledgments

All photos were taken by me, except as noted below.

> The photos on pages 18, 26, 32, and 49 are courtesy of my uncle Giorgio Mobili (Sr.).
>
> The photo on page 58 is courtesy of Savo Vulević.
>
> The photo on page 74 is courtesy of my father Gianni Mobili.
>
> The photo on page 92 I took in January, 2020 at the GAM cultural center in Santiago, Chile. It represents a politically charged mural by Javier Barraza (@jebarvi).
>
> The photo on page 95 is courtesy of Carlo Pagliughi.

Poems *Sirens, Sicilian Renaissance, American Casanova, Perfect Sleep, The Grownup Years, Fear of Heights, Horoscope, Pledge,* and *Quinta Vergara* are English versions of Italian poems from my last two Italian collections, *Miracoli ed effetti* (Pèquod, 2016) and *Dimenticare un hotel* (Puntoacapo, 2020).

Although the themes explored in this collection are of a piece with the ones I have extensively frequented in my Italian production, the idea of writing a poetry book (my first) directly in English grew out of a series of musical conversations/happenings with Jaime Rodríguez Matos, whom I thank dearly for his input.

Many thanks to editor Marc Estrin for prompting me to envision a photographic counterpart to what was originally a poetry-only manuscript. My heartfelt thanks also to Donna Bister for her beautiful layout work, and for her patience putting up with my incessant last-minute image shuffles.

And lastly, thanks to Gloria Medina Sancho, as usual, for her keen eye and wise counsel.

Sunken Boulevards

The Scent of Tomorrow

We must inhabit the fringes
where emptiness rings as thin as a pin drop
the more we pull back, the more it will bleed
(let amnesia be the kindest mutilation)

The special ferocity of courtyards
thirty years too late:
where nothing has grown, can we still hold our noses
and call it our own?

These are the scents of tomorrow
everybody here can sweat a little English
no need to shanghai the lead
into a shimmering crevice, behind the radio shop
to hunt down with slingshots the footsteps of our withdrawal
from promise-filled kitchens
(or the festering thing within us
that voided them all).

What We Leave Behind

Say the names again, tonight
the ones that kept us going
through shadowy columns
in angles of flight
Renée Doratiotto, Verónica Martí
Carlo Alberto Parisi...
our soft dreams well-fed
when we hunched over textbooks of stone
asmolder with kingly temptations
with no intuition
no concept at all of the pull
of dry days ahead.

What's your favorite kiss à la carte?
You'd love me to hush and unwind
but the measure is full
the season is dead
and I'm fading from every plate
leaving nothing behind.

Lovers Gone Wrong

Just when we could have chiseled the chain
here come the cow-faced
stampeding on our fingers:
lovers gone wrong in manners untold
brewing their ills
in back of ancient stonework.

It's the end of time at the Ostia waterfront
naked under the stars
gleam black-hearted computations…

It isn't hard to misunderstand us
the way we stumbled into this frame
from the sidewalk
crooking the house, burning the orchard
testing ourselves to see
if the heart still fractures
when all we longed for was
(on that station platform)
to lay down our horns and weapons
and disappear at last
onto the next empty train.

Go West

"Enough tampering with ghosts
I like to travel light"
then you rushed back inside
to get rid of the rest:
the curtains, the meadow, the blue books
a quick rubber kiss on the asphalt
from your Prancing Fool.

(She picks up and reads
and continues to bear West
for the Whirlpool of sun-blasted Nowhere...)

Yet our timing for failure was off
when you ran my finger on the seam:
a twist of the eye and the mystery fades
no more smoothing the teeth marks
in the stuff of our dream.

Revelation

I faked my last revelation
so you'd believe
all the others I have sworn by.
Previously unseen in our monochrome skies...
Try as you might
it won't stop harmonizing:
we surface from darkness
with nothing but cherry bombs
to end without gain on the sunken
border of dawn.

Stick a hair
between jamb and door
lie in wait for the return of your old flame
join the blank faces at Lido Café—
or we could inch along to some
radical endgame:
burn the memory tree
turn your back on the lit-up room
ride the dangerous streets of chance and larceny
to the edge of the moon.

Vacancy

We were the last ones at the beach
with no one left to call
except an inch behind the curtains
the lady on the brink
who had returned to end it all.

She carried her furious death song
to all who would listen
then cracked into vaporous beams
like a strafe-bombed café…

On the strength of an elegant scheme
I break and enter without cost
but the chairs have leafed out
a ghost stands at the sink:
there are no busier rooms
than the ones we have lost.

Seasonal Heartbreak

You promise you won't—back away
from the chafing, tough skin of remembrance
steel me against your best color wheel
then break my back with someone
else's bag of niceties…

Yet we shattered the rules of longing
the night we strayed and let the town digest us
into its damp summer air.

Tied to his post, the supplicant weaves
a red canopy for our shining dependencies
millions of hearts believe they are whole
taking for granted
each step of assembly.

So much wreckage has come between us
and no ambassador, god, or kind officiator
of a polished retreat.

Different Birds

No decapitating birds
attempted to compete
with the tightness of tungsten, the malice of steel.
If we hide in these ruined baths
there's no proof that we exist:
won't our looming portfolios
revert to dust?

We embraced at the gateway
under planetary good cheer
then bright / hot / saturate / green glow
the point where you looked back and waved...

Unreadable lips
papers blow in the street:
pick them up to keep memory afloat
in the day that recedes.

Hinterland

Trumped-up falls on the school grounds
sharpness hiding in the weeds
Bakelite soldiers on the living-room floor
there is nothing to save
if you can't break free—of the hinterland.

Take a quick look in the mirror
check if your chin is still there
it's safer to picture what you can't touch or see
have your darkest fears
dribble in through the blinds—in the hinterland.

Peripheral lovers entangled
their raincoats flapping on the rails
darting little details we must forget to live on
shriveled in the west
spinning webs of return—to the hinterland.

Back To Bonera

Say we come back—to Bonera
as summer hastens its cold liquidations
crystallized blood brings no sharks
all wetness subsumed into the atmosphere...

Sweet memories flock to gum up visibility
the mystery of breaking
when the reasons for not breaking
were the soundest in years.

The future takes hold—like an illness
we get quite cunning in our waning days
spinning high-flown ruminations
about what fails
in spite of good intentions...

On these steps we once planned
to hit the French Riviera
but agents unknown deployed their stony fingers
on things softer than stone.

Heartbreak Café

Fire feels colder—and safer
than my troubles with you
I listen but seek confirmation
in the drift of your knees.

As the silence of sidewalks endangers our perimeter
we keep up the act and words spiral down
like pressed flowers from books.

Someone says, "Water plus eye
equals crying in Chinese…"
It's open mic on mortality
everyone's face hangs from hooks.

But nobody knows for sure how many tears were shed
how many hearts are closed for restoration
at Heartbreak Café.

Sirens

Look at him: the general weary of leisure
shuffles down the street
the conifers sway and the women
pack his bags for the journey to another virgin shore
make a plea to the demons of camouflage
distill with his spirits the mirages
that will see him through.

Don't you see?
every article worthy of allegiance
has remained right here
in the fogs that shaped our complexion:
now the impossible beaches give way under our feet
all the wins and defeats file into our dreams
and missing in the middle
the siren that once bade us leave.

CHINA

So many hours poured into this bedroom
and when the last came
no one was there to warn us
not the condemned rollercoaster
not the rearview Virgin
with the cobalt blue shiner...

We kissed on the threshold as everything was fading
no consummate arbitrator of sad atmospheres
could have cut through this gloom.

Come to the spots that won't recognize you
watch them at nighttime
or through a dead pool of sunblaze.

Blinds should be drawn for the mind's shears
to slash the dark inside
into boundless partitions:
like the sparkling embrace of china
when visits dragged on too long to mean anything
other than time without end.

Starve Game

Should I disown my own bed
all interface between my mouth and this starve game
free of the drone that poisons the land
to rise up for air, far away from all ruin?

Find my fabulous youth again
a steady voltage
the swishing cape of secret assignations
at the local café...

There is a woman on Ventura
like a cold snap from the slopes of Antarctica
buttons and brooches have worn thin
she's sown a little piece of death in our garden...

Now the evenings crack open edgewise
and I can see the cut, but for reasons
that remain until the end
ferociously dim.

Cocktails

The onlookers arch their backs
up against the new release, short-shrifting
the cocktails, *the glories of Greece*
commands and no more binding voices
to burn them on the skin
high trumpets of centuries past (as if what was
hadn't always been losing itself
under smooth glass…)

A cool sleight of hand
has bent the measure of our days
to the riddle of what streets to walk on
for how long, by what name.

Home

It's pouring time
the house at the end of the evening
yawns into the stars
we crowd every absence of purpose
relentless and cruel
in skewering your shallow American glimmer
the resilience of your next ride out.

Pointless words
when darkness gains on us humans
(perhaps we're not alone)
in the name of what—that is colder?

One more night on the road
and tomorrow we'll be dreaming
of reasons to batter
the castle that we called our home.

CRASH LANDING

Hidden in crisp Sunday greens
can you sense it—the escape we never mastered?
Tossed all four suits from the jail train
Thou shalt be cast out, so our past is safe again...

Watch those fugitives on their faceless helicopters:
could this really be our way
out of the paradise
where you can't be asleep?

When my tongue feels too much like muscle
I let the aching heart burn itself to cinders
no smooth productions, no artsy moons
not even a pass key to break into your bedroom...

I wear the wrong face for this time zone
still airborne, true
but headed for hard pavement
in a cold neighborhood.

Heatwave

Summer dismembers to the bone
nothing's concealed
that won't shine on your forehead
the brochures announce the Thing in itself
a place to exhale with few lighting misjudgments.

Some pay for their pleasures
yet the pickings are short and slim:
pretty girls of poor stock
keep them clear of the check points
and they might soften your chin.

Gentlemen deem it uncouth
for a troubadour to wail beneath her window
but to desist, is to dissipate
like a puddle of joy in the mouth of a heatwave...

At night we wait for sleep to stir our legs of stone
so we can leave this table and keep shunning
what we've been aching for.

Summer Songs

Welcome the chance to gather your pickings
thirty years on
at Park Gallanti Village
so many numbers, no one to reach
with the two-pronged whip
of gratitude and anger.

Nothing beckons
beyond the infantry of sponge rocks
but there's a discount on breathing
if you hold your peace
and hide the growth on your hand.

Deny we've ever been here before
let each gesture
recoup its primal splendor
the lazy chartings across the sand
the electric nights to uncouple need from longing...

We'll give our doubles free pennies for the juke box
we'll pay three weepers to watch them dance
in tears, to the old summer songs.

Intercom

The kettle is on: grind some beans.
Let the aroma take care of the elements.
Folks here don't care much—for thinking:
they know how seasons can instigate their coattails
to fill like sails beyond the bounds of reason
until the streets are empty
or flooded in phosphorus half-veils...

State your name right into the box
no one will answer
yet metal might move for you.
Surplus politeness from before
and nothing to bind it to the face of tomorrow:
to whether it's still there hanging
from fictions as dogged as tough yellowed string
at the end of your drawer.

Boundless Hotels

Let the sparrows sanctify
the gas pumps and the fling
keeping fear on her good side:
then first in the cordage of morning
servants will bitch of their lot
by the left wing...

Boundless hotels
solder your fantasy of escape
to a crack in the window:
hold it suspect
as you search for the right ear
to inform on this night ride
under no obligation
to mimic the language of aliens...

We make stranger sounds
each time we dream of an alcove
winnowed from absence
a rosary wound for our black thoughts.

Sicilian Renaissance

Take a nice stroll in the piazza
and your troubles will graciously linger
on the shaded side of the wall
set to pounce—should the safety net flounder.

Free your cheer from all hope and longing
no retrospection, no picking at the lesions
you're professing to heal.

If Giuni Russo were here
her birdsong—a cold shower to the lovelorn
these halls of shame would go up
at her signal, in one seigniorial bonfire:
all the blue Monets shot to Venus...

But we're wrong again if we kill it
only so that its memory
continues to breathe.

Day of Reckoning

What will remain on the page
once the *I said / he said* gets blue-penciled
what will be leaned on, perused
how many clean chances
to whitewash our bruises...

We were burning against the landscape:
you said, "The workers are going to hell
waving their shiny magic wands!"
I was charting your lips.

Where will you be the next time around
still holding court
on the very day of reckoning
keeping the bum notes out of your sound
feeding the thin glow between door and lintel...

Until we see the stone arches crumble
at piece with our foreignness, at long last
under a blanket of chips.

Tahiti

It was my last September night
with Verónica Martí
Father quotes from the paper:
The Revolt of the Sea...
about our secret flight plan to Tahiti
on Uncle's motorboat
no one is callous enough
to speak or laugh...

We picnicked on the roof
watching the backhoes kick up dust.

We've been troublesome guests to our lodgers:
now the boulevards sink
thieves are sentenced to crawl
even now there's no shorthand retreat
from this tumbling wall.

Closing Time

In my last guard-rail confession
one name recurred: Elizabeth del Carlo
never disown a trail that is cold
(and even if you do, who might be there to hear it?)

Must the abandoned train station
be included in the body count—
any act unperformed
expounded as due reticence?

Study the ancient drag marks
collect what lingers
 in wrought-iron elevators
(someone is crying on the roof of your house
something was burning
at the center of my bedroom...)

At closing time we polish up our memories
let our hollows put on the gracious camouflage
of what cannot return.

Victims of Stars

It's all over, Georgie boy
you know it all too well, there is nothing
to hope for, you've got nothing to sell.
She's safe in her platinum ribcage
six hundred stories high:
try to keep your composure
as you watch her rise.

Behold the poor victims of stars
blue aeroliths in the twilight
until one small-lettered day
they forsake what they've spun for
for a whistle that can't be called human
the chemical pull to the hard floor
of a room at the edge of the world
past the old iron gate.

American Casanova

Under the purchase of this motionless horizon
no suitor will expose his chin to abuse
in the cold iron of a morning, not one chamber
will maintain the same coordinates as on his prior call.

Of his victories (besides the immortal song)
only whispered names and domiciles
are left before a languid fiscal court: Samantha Truong
Elizabeth Del Carlo, Chiara Hildebrandt
Verónica Martí, Nicole Coviello
forty-three fifteen Contessa, seven ninety West Ventura
Selma, Porterville, Merced, Santa Clarita, California.

As we push our watermelon carts down endless avenues
we cannot bear to put the myth to rest
of reckless flights through nurseries and gallows
performed by gallant lovers in disguise.

Chickens

Only strangers can go in
that's why it glows like jade
but in spite of the bright crew
the chickens will cross where it's dim
caught in a hermeneutic cage
like that hovel we shared near the station
when no one had trained us
to see what unfolds
under each layer of blue.

Still I hopped on the fast train
as if my fate depended on the speed
watched Milan peel away
like a wretch on a tumbrel, retreat
to a capsule of cold
in a land without rain.

Rekindling

Make the swallows disappear
cold spirals of hindsight
around the passage of our years
when coffee contained all the molds
and love was the church in a heatwave...

Now I'm back in Milan unprepared
to encounter a fissure
a window, a fold
where nothing used to be...

But suppose the big marbles stand guard
over the fumes of past flagellations
the place is still lit
your gaze crosses mine:
who's to say that my yellow papers
can't be another's fool's gold?

Perfect Sleep

Then came the days of quiet despair
relentless on the dogs
no incentive to leave for defectors
but dreams—that sweet pollen of angels...

Not far from the big homes
with the good spirits and the rugs
the old cosmodrome retains
all secret intents: mine, too, can be seen
sapping the hardness of steel.

Under your bedclothes
hum the five proofs that God exists
by brother Aquinas, trusted convector
in the cold pre-electrical mists:
feel their spark, even now, in your feet
as you fall
into your perfect sleep.

Feathers

You'd like to be pierced—like Teresa
but my feathers are goose
(no one survives in these regions
without hair on their skin...)

There's an interdict on every strong intention
yet the mind keeps spinning despite clear admonitions
that the moorings are loose.

I leave no words: please, don't listen
for my voice—in the reeds
let the white meltdown of eternity
fill in the hole of your grief...

"Very well, thanks" you'll say when asked about your sanity
the language we spoke preserved for future scrutiny
in the annals of birds.

The Grownup Years

The streets feigned indifference
but for a gang of God's fools
all the creatures we forget to hold dear
half-asleep behind their rage.

We kissed goodbye
after our gig at the Funk
still reeling from the contretemps
(how that stranger had to stand up and sneer
when I opened your cage)

We drove back through a universe
of microscopic agents in suits
bent on effacing everyone's trail of tears
of youthful spunk
the stage long set for the silence
of our grownup years.

The Call

The hours we dropped on lost avenues
never made any sound hitting stone
yet we cover our ears to be fashionable
bending backwards—as we're told.
Sometimes a face bleeds sepia
over frostbite, to sweeten the deal
but when nights are hot
all the locks are cold
under the great Cinzano doll…

We're the same old frames without shadow
as we pace up and down the lobby
hunters, shepherds, gigolos
crushed by the stillness of telephone poles.

Some keep dreaming in this twilight
of giving themselves to the call.

Radioland

You tried to warn me: I just kept the radio on
the frog on the billboard
declared the healing had begun:
to rise for air, one extra mile
a rush for seats.

We sat on the shore
waiting for wingèd words from home
the dark patch still gleaming
and no one else to sponge it down:
you'd blow up screens with your castaway smile
no need to go underground.

The farther we run
the more raveled the pain
the more we hold on to—still hold on to
this stupid refrain.

Night Ride

She feels every counter-step
on the gravel like the sound of a clock
at this hour the pure substance of fright
is seeping into her walk.

On the road you don't wonder
whether it's God's will
(there might still be humans to blame)
never think it could happen to you
hewing so close to the flame.

Don't ask for the true word
we must insist that it stay out of reach
against the outfit that hunts down and kills
every absence of goal
take this nothing—stretch it tight
and string it through your soul.

Black Heart

In time the reasons not to rise
sharpen up on the landscape's wall
your headstrong ways, your Red Guard livery
find a pretty shelf to rest them on...

She made it very clear for you
that double voice that nourishes:
"you'll waste away
on the arm of a courteous kind..."

April is the last good king
before the puppet rule of July:
spring clean your brittle heart
no need to know how empty it ever was
that hole beneath your skin—blacker than coal
that hole beneath your white skin
blacker than cold, stormy night.

Diva

The heiress looks nice
she gives her nod on the radio
amid ratcheting sounds
resembling gunfire.

On sunken screens, the Magi
line up to kiss her hand
we might come to regret our dance
but the ruse enchants us tonight.

Then suddenly—*fever*
turns the tables on all the axes
(you never looked paler
what is muddying up your glow?)

Staple your stance
to the hem of your silk hose.
Run for the stars, you belong to everyone:
to every believer
whom misfortune has laid low.

Night Song

Beneath night's stifling currents
what has fouled all libations
now can simulate mornings
with windup refrains...

You were right to board the windows
I must rest here on the sidewalk
like a spent necromancer
unsure of the dark
lord it over the monkeys
and all creatures that scuttle:

under these cold conditions
will you still hear my love
plucking strings
as I stamp my foot
on the ground?

Lockdown

Secure all doors and windows
as the last kind guest rounds the corner
to bleed out over the asphalt
of Memory Street...

Bring back the days of hunger
the evenings of warm misdirection
(if you chose the straight and narrow
you'll never reach port)

Did you leave a light turned on
and loose change in the plant pot
strictly for lovers that may know
the right thing to do?

Ghosts scamper in the chimney
break out your rock paper scissors
you know they'll never settle
for a dignified truce.

Fear Of Heights

Remember that morning at the rock
you and I and Toni Martí
the sky held no promise of mercy or rain
still we waived the referee.

There was a sharp clap down on the pavement
followed by a distant scamper
I shook from my head to the quick of my soul
until she clamped one on my knee…

Now we ride the gusts of bad dreaming
knowing that the unscripted reasons
have withered away with their old domains
and our debentures—set in gold
keep us sheltered from His judgment
without ever granting release.

Friendly Fire

What spreads through the firmament
when you hang up on friends and foes
you feel like a vengeance machine
as you swallow the phone.

What chafes at your fancy
in the wee small hours, I doubt
you would recognize:
our face has an end of days look
when the angle is right.

It's midnight uptown and the sidewalks shine
white as elephant's tusks:
before the rumble of traffic returns
to snuff out desire
swing me high, rock me sweet
wrap me tight in friendly fire.

Boat of Return

No one was the same
after watching your new simulation
of the heatwaves and the pains
in the long drought to come:
we swear like weathered sea wolves
but even in the kindest waters
the hull of our future
will gather darkness and rust.

From a ghastly symphony
of seething space turning inward
we gleaned we should have paid more heed
to the voice in the clouds.

Now gone is the lift that sustained us
on fairy's breath vapors
and stranded still—our little boat of return.

Borderline

Everything *except this black*
I can cede without turning into rock
or any bitter cold hard thing:
I'm growing my sea legs, recasting my rings.

We set to tasks below the spirit's nether fringe
we trimmed our sails
to catch each novelty breeze
and the raincoat draped over the pain
they say it only came to me
through some unreported wreck...

We veiled our purpose to the hilt
because of our soft romantic spine:
but any truancy from the straight path
would not have changed a thing
beyond this borderline.

Horoscope

Now she refrains, in the evenings
courting a cosmic—catastrophe
at night a black sky puts them under
without the grace of a horoscope...

They call on some god to dust off ancient statutes
it helps that he only stalks the pretty memories
and the gilding is free.

Conflict, you cry, breaks the soul
(touching the onion to the eyes and soft skin)
here are my spoils, Lacedaemonian
nourish your fire
let me plume over the city
for inside and out the ground is what it ever was
an open terrain of ruses and defections
and we abide by its laws.

Summer Days

There will be more summer days
spaces to pace off and leave at one's leisure
alien indulgence will plant
soluble proof among last wills and photos:
and street lamps will snap on like when we used to need them
the same tiny creatures will land on the wisteria
to cast a spell on our sleep.

In dream we hug—the walls of buildings
until forgotten sounds waft out of their windows
sometimes we go deeper, where doors don't hang right
and the hand tucking us in may be
that of our enemy
old faces are shrouded in a milky sheen
and fingers can't touch, yet dangerously
spark trouble in time.

Night Chill

We fancied ourselves scot-free
when everything closed off in misery
a murmur shook us from the inside
or was it a chill
from a long-forgotten dream?

We swore to leave it where it was
and go stare at it—on tiptoes:
but when it comes down to the milk streets
you can never know
how fast it grows...

From the northernmost catastrophes of bliss
what's a little more crash and burn?

"Come stand on this ledge"—He said
"Lord it over the remains
force the ghosts to will again."

Nightwatchers

Don't toss your graces to the dogs
he won't reward any bomb-throwing disguise
he would rather be touched
with a ten-foot flower
and have you blend in with the wall.

You lie awake, holding nothing
burned by the rope of obstruction
speculative hearts feel the two are one
but yours shall smolder
till you're gone.

We nurse our drink in dank corners
feeding on the shock of summer
watch another night shatter on shards of want
(where you bleed, there we will be)

What's a fair price for our troubles
deferring the light spear of dawn?

Pledge

Behold the children of summer
how they drop their inkwells and run
flouting all gravitational straits
this time we won't be outdone.

Concierges of sad hotels
the vanity of sunlight
we'll twist into a screen for your plays
to nurse under burgundy shades
the incurable hurt of love and regret.

On the walls of the Excelsior
we'll chisel every known counterfact
we'll separate insurgents from louts
and the damsels above
court in rhymeless verse
from the languorous asphalts of fall.

Boys

This hole in the ground was the school
where we glued our Savior to the flue
then squirmed through the clicks
of a rotary game, as yellow chips
kept tumbling from the sky...

Sometimes a road uncluttered
glimmered in a cloud of curtains
yet the mystery train must be missed and missed
for us boys to grow fond of our lot.

We swear, "This is not my number"
spar with our tall enablers
spurn everyone's right to a second shot
at their only good reason to spare:
but when night gains on the twilight
you'll find us incessantly there.

Return To Villa Severi

Remember that night at Villa Severi
the four wise men setting up
a crime scene diamond.
We lingered to watch the yellow unspool
relentlessly, like the sash on our chipped bond.

You said: "Truth is, I never"— then muddled up the closure
I said: "I beg your pardon"—expecting no forgiveness
after the body was gone.

When our motives end up forgotten
suppose it's merely the second-worst solution.
What took us down had no axes to grind
and even failure, sometimes
might lose steam on the right floor…

No fabulous tailspins
no one-armed reassurances
no glittering hopes tonight, as I silently return
to knock on your door.

Charcoal Beaches

"If you only knew
what cold, intractable darkness
you are putting me through..."
Then my high ground started to crumble
as the tail of our words cut a supersonic path
to the seafront hotels we forgot to leave, as if
in the cracks of a curtain
the ossified could breathe anew.

False alarm:
there goes the work of a lifetime
down the kitchen sink
up in warm spirals of hindsight...

What is it *that is not*, and yet casts a glimmer
on charcoal beaches we can't terraform—
the dream that informed us
still hanging from your corset strings.

Narrow Margins

The story stays reluctant, no meat
behind the surface of what we did.

Stranger raps on our bedroom window
a chance to track down our flights
from service: *board it up, shut it down.*

We dusted every footprint our father left
in courtyards, on empty streets:
blood is dry down the grass embankment
paper said she was safe in Reno
let the quiet Gringo, one last time
save the day.

Narrow down what you can't remember
were we killed in our Sunday stupor
or were we up, fully awake
with plenty of escape?

Dark

The old castle's silhouette
presiding over throngs
never hard or unsmiling
in the jaws of regret
secured to their spot
in the arras of space-time...

Even stout hearts tonight
had to yield to the white slurp
that punched all the air out of Calle Colón
befouling our view of Miss Wong
the pizzazz in her sails...

Let the castle's embrace
keep us in oxygen and dreams
until fabulous men are assembled
(the modified breed of a flatfoot)
to meet this new frightening
call of the dark.

Sunken Boulevards

The rain cools the heartbreak
then lust sows its snails in the hedges
astride the red condor
it's you, the blonde, and the moon.

Call from a phone booth
declare scorched earth on your bygones
pack up your stockings
and run away with the swoon...

"There's only one awake", says
the flickering lamppost: "the contour
of a door, the old man at the bar."

Will a sunken boulevard
float your colors forever?
There's no falling when you cling
to your dearest mistake.

Quinta Vergara

Now that daylight prefers to linger
in the other room
all our dead gardens will blossom
once more in dreams...

This cold town—great despoiler
of many a gentle afternoon
is it really the face
of what we've become?

Don't take it to heart
if I won't be coming back
even now that the old fences have come down...

For what is keeping us apart
is our ultimate defense:
the grace that persists
in what might have been.

About the Author

Giorgio Mobili is a poet, translator, and literary critic. Born in Milan, Italy, he has lived in the US since 1999. He teaches Humanities and Spanish at California State University, Fresno. In his lyrical production, he has persistently explored, from a multi-lingual perspective, and with surrealistic flair, how cultural displacement reshapes one's inner geography through the intricate mobilization of memory, fantasy, and desire. His Italian poetry has appeared in several journals and five published collections, and has been included in the anthology *Poets of the Italian Diaspora* (Fordham University Press, 2014). His first Spanish-language collection came out in Santiago, Chile, in 2014. His English poetry has appeared in *The Tipton Poetry Journal*, *Pank Magazine*, *The Hiram Poetry Review*, *Ariel*, and *Gradiva*. This is his first full-length collection in English.

Fomite

More poetry from Fomite...

Anna Blackmer — *Hexagrams*
L. Brown — *Loopholes*
Sue D. Burton — *Little Steel*
Christine Butterworth-McDermott — *Evelyn As*
David Cavanagh— *Cycling in Plato's Cave*
James Connolly — *Picking Up the Bodies*
Greg Delanty — *Loosestrife*
Mason Drukman — *Drawing on Life*
J. C. Ellefson — *Foreign Tales of Exemplum and Woe*
Anna Faktorovich — *Improvisational Arguments*
Barry Goldensohn — *Snake in the Spine, Wolf in the Heart*
Barry Goldensohn — *The Hundred Yard Dash Man*
Barry Goldensohn — *The Listener Aspires to the Condition of Music*
Barry Goldensohn — *Visitors Entrance*
R. L. Green — *When You Remember Deir Yassin*
KJ Hannah Greenberg — *Beast There—Don't That*
Gail Holst-Warhaft — *Lucky Country*
Judith Kerman — *Definitions*
Joseph Lamport — *Enlightenment*
Raymond Luczak — *A Babble of Objects*
Kate Magill — *Roadworthy Creature, Roadworthy Craft*
Tony Magistrale — *Entanglements*
Gary Mesick — *General Discharge*
Giorgio Mobili — *Sunken Boulevards*
Andreas Nolte — *Mascha: The Poems of Mascha Kaléko*
Sherry Olson — *Four-Way Stop*
Brett Ortler — *Lessons of the Dead*
David Polk — *Drinking the River*
Janice Miller Potter — *Meanwell*
Janice Miller Potter — *Thoreau's Umbrella*
Philip Ramp — *Arrivals and Departures*
Philip Ramp — *The Melancholy of a Life as the Joy of Living It Slowly Chills*
Joseph D. Reich — *A Case Study of Werewolves*
Joseph D. Reich — *Connecting the Dots to Shangrila*
Joseph D. Reich — *The Derivation of Cowboys and Indians*
Joseph D. Reich — *The Hole That Runs Through Utopia*
Joseph D. Reich — *The Housing Market*
Kenneth Rosen and Richard Wilson — *Gomorrah*
Fred Rosenblum — *Playing Chicken with an Iron Horse*
Fred Rosenblum — *Tramping Solo*
Fred Rosenblum — *Vietnumb*
David Schein — *My Murder and Other Local News*
Harold Schweizer — *Miriam's Book*
Scott T. Starbuck — *Carbonfish Blues*

Fomite

Scott T. Starbuck — *Hawk on Wire*
Scott T. Starbuck — *Industrial Oz*
Seth Steinzor — *Among the Lost*
Seth Steinzor — *Once Was Lost*
Seth Steinzor — *To Join the Lost*
Susan Thomas — *In the Sadness Museum*
Susan Thomas — *Silent Acts of Public Indiscretion*
Susan Thomas — *The Empty Notebook Interrogates Itself*
Sharon Webster — *Everyone Lives Here*
Tony Whedon — *The Très Riches Heures*
Tony Whedon — *The Falkland Quartet*
Claire Zoghb — *Dispatches from Everest*

Dual Language

Vito Bonito/Alison Grimaldi Donahue — *Soffiata Via/Blown Away*
Antonello Borra/Blossom Kirschenbaum — *Alfabestiario*
Antonello Borra/Blossom Kirschenbaum — *AlphaBetaBestiario*
Antonello Borra/Anis Memon — *Fabbrica delle idee/The Factory of Ideas*
Tina Escaja/Mark Eisner — *Caída Libre/Free Fall*
Luigi Fontanella/Giorgio Mobili — *L'adolescenza e la notte/Adolescence and Night*
Aristea Papalexandrou/Philip Ramp — *Μας προσπερνά/It's Overtaking Us*
Katerina Anghelaki-Rooke//Philip Ramp — *Losing Appetite for Existence*
Jeannette Clariond/Lawrence Schimel — *Desert Memory*
Mikis Theodoraksi/Gail Holst-Warhaft — *The House with the Scorpions*
Paolo Valesio/Todd Portnowitz — *La Mezzanotte di Spoleto/Midnight in Spoleto*

Writing a review on social media sites for readers will help the progress of independent publishing. To submit a review, go to the book page on any of the sites and follow the links for reviews. Books from independent presses rely on reader-to-reader communications.

For more information or to order any of our books, visit:
http://www.fomitepress.com/our-books.html

www.ingramcontent.com/pod-product-compliance
Lightning Source LLC
Chambersburg PA
CBHW071420070526
44578CB00003B/634